CREATE YOUR OWN LOG BOOK EXAMPLES

Create your own Log Book with this easy-to-use 7 Column Log Book. You can find below a couple of examples of how to create Column Headers for different needs.

Ledger Book, Income and Expenses Log Book or Accounts Book

Create a Ledger Book to track your Income and Expenses easily so that you can stay in control of your finances. Use the following prompts as column headers:

NO	DATE	DESCRIPTION	ACCOUNT	INCOME	EXPENSE	TOTAL

Accounting Ledger Book

Create an Accounting Ledger Book to track easily finances and transactions. Use the following prompts as column headers:

NO	DATE	DESCRIPTION	ACCOUNT	DEBIT	CREDIT	BALANCE

Petty Cash Log Book

Create a Petty Cash Log Book to easily track your cash flow. Use the following prompts as column headers:

NO	DATE	DETAIL	CASH IN	CASH OUT	BALANCE	NOTES

Inventory and Equipment Log Book

Create an Inventory and Equipment Log Book to easily track inventory and equipment. Use the following prompts as column headers:

NO	DATE	ITEM DESCRIPTION	QUANTITY	PRICE	LOCATION	NOTES

Online Order Book

Create an Online Order Book to easily track online purchases. Use the following prompts as column headers:

NO	DATE	ITEM DESCRIPTION	ORDER #	COMPANY	AMOUNT	RECEIVED DATE

Vehicle Maintenance Log Book

Create a Vehicle Maintenance Log Book to easily track maintenance and repair. Use the following prompts as column headers:

DAY	DATE	DESCRIPTION OF WORK DONE	MILEAGE	LOCATION/ COMPANY	REPLACEMENT PARTS	COST

Mileage Log Book

Create a Mileage Log Book to easily track vehicle gas usage for tax reporting purposes. Use the following prompts as column headers:

DATE	TIME	DESTINATION	ODOMETER START	ODOMETER END	TOTAL MILEAGE	NOTES

Donation Log Book

Create a Donation Log Book to easily track charitable donations. Use the following prompts as column headers:

NO	DATE GIVEN	ORGANIZATION/ INDIVIDUAL NAME AND DETAILS	DONATION (CASH, ITEMS)	VALUE	PAYMENT METHOD	TAX (Y/N) DEDUCTIBLE

Visitor Log Book

Create a Visitor Log Book to keep track of office guests and factory, company visitors. Use the following prompts as column headers:

NO	DATE	VISITOR'S NAME	REASON FOR VISIT	TIME IN	TIME OUT	SIGN/INITIAL

Daily Activity Log Book

Create a Daily Activity Log Book to easily track your daily activities, appointments, tasks or contacts. Use the following prompts as column headers:

DAY	DATE	APPOINMENT, TASK, OR CONTACT	START TIME	END TIME	TOTAL TIME	COMPLETED

Time Sheet Log Book

Create a Time Sheet Log Book to keep track of daily work hours, have everything in order, and get paid accordingly. Use the following prompts as column headers:

DAY	DATE	DESCRIPTION	TIME IN	TIME OUT	TOTAL HOURS	NOTES

Blood Pressure Log Book

Create a Blood Pressure Log Book to easily track your blood pressure signs. Use the following prompts as column headers:

DAY	DATE	NOTES	TIME	SYSTOLIC	DIASTOLIC	HEART RATE

Blood Sugar Log Book

Create a Blood Sugar Log Book to keep track of your blood sugar levels. Use the following prompts as column headers:

DAY	DATE	NOTES	MEAL	BEFORE	AFTER	DOSE

